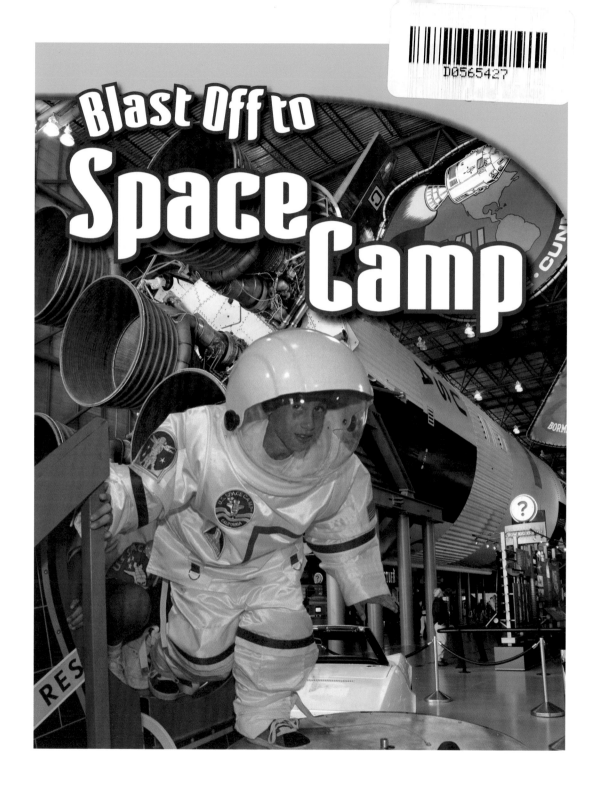

Blast Off to Space Camp

Hillary Wolfe

Consultant

Timothy Rasinski, Ph.D.
Kent State University

Publishing Credits

Dona Herweck Rice, *Editor-in-Chief*

Robin Erickson, *Production Director*

Lee Aucoin, *Creative Director*

Conni Medina, M.A.Ed., *Editorial Director*

Jamey Acosta, *Editor*

Heidi Kellenberger, *Editor*

Lexa Hoang, *Designer*

Lesley Palmer, *Designer*

Stephanie Reid, *Photo Editor*

Rachelle Cracchiolo, M.S.Ed., *Publisher*

Teacher Created Materials

5301 Oceanus Drive
Huntington Beach, CA 92649-1030
http://www.tcmpub.com

ISBN 978-1-4333-3673-7

© 2012 Teacher Created Materials, Inc.

Table of Contents

Welcome to Space Camp!

When you think of camp, do you picture campfires and tents? That's one kind of camp. But there is another type of camp—space camp! A scientist named Wernher von Braun (VAIR-ner von BROUN) saw band camps, football camps, and cheerleading camps. He wondered why there weren't science camps. He wanted to give children the chance to see what it would be like to be an **astronaut** (AS-truh-nawt).

◄ Space campers test a rocket.

▲ studying the solar system

U.S. Space and Rocket Center

The U.S. Space and Rocket Center is a space museum located in Huntsville, Alabama. People visit the museum from all over the world to learn about space exploration and see the restored *Saturn V* (SAT-ern FAHYV) moon rocket.

His dream came true in 1982. That is when the first space camp opened in Huntsville, Alabama. Now there are space camps in many cities. Many museums and **planetariums** (plan-i-TAIR-ee-uhmz) offer space camps, too.

Planetariums

A planetarium is a theater that projects images of stars, planets, and other heavenly bodies on a dome-shaped ceiling. Planetariums offer shows to teach about astronomy.

What to Expect

When you arrive, you'll check in and meet the counselors. Each student gets a log book. A log book is a type of journal in which campers can record everything they see and do. Astronauts and pilots keep log books, too.

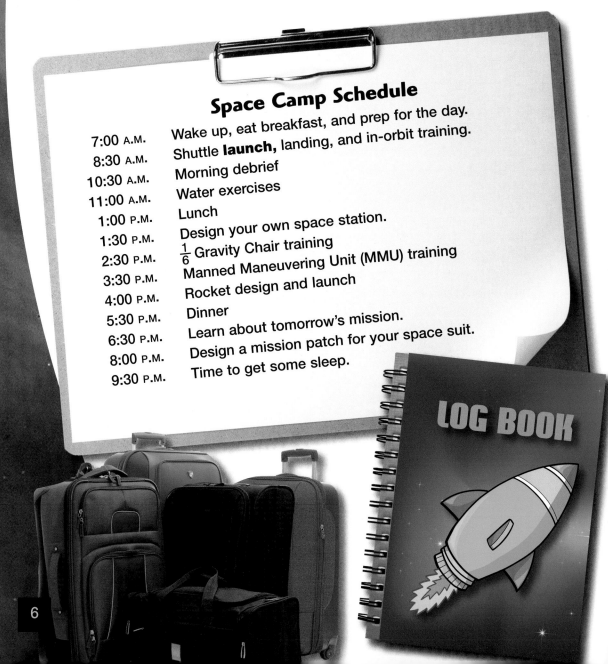

Space Camp Schedule

Time	Activity
7:00 A.M.	Wake up, eat breakfast, and prep for the day.
8:30 A.M.	Shuttle **launch,** landing, and in-orbit training.
10:30 A.M.	Morning debrief
11:00 A.M.	Water exercises
1:00 P.M.	Lunch
1:30 P.M.	Design your own space station.
2:30 P.M.	$\frac{1}{6}$ Gravity Chair training
3:30 P.M.	Manned Maneuvering Unit (MMU) training
4:00 P.M.	Rocket design and launch
5:30 P.M.	Dinner
6:30 P.M.	Learn about tomorrow's mission.
8:00 P.M.	Design a mission patch for your space suit.
9:30 P.M.	Time to get some sleep.

LOG BOOK

While you're there, you will need to get used to using space lingo. The water fountain is called the *H_2O dispenser*. The bathroom is called *waste management*. The living spaces are *habitats*. When they arrive, students head to their habitats to stow their gear in *sleeping bays*.

from the journal of astronaut Sandra Magus aboard the International Space ▼ ▶

Sandra Magnus' Journal
A Typical Day

I am going to try to describe a typical day of life on the ISS. Many people have asked this question, I imagine wondering what everyday life is like in such an unusual place and environment. First and foremost I need to point out that our days, all of them, are planned by a huge, world-wide group of people on the ground. The planning for an increment (ours is Expedition 18, for example) actually starts up to a year in advance. The long term planners from every country get together and start mapping out how to fit in all of the work priorities that everyone has. These priorities can range from installing new equipment, getting certain science experiments done, getting maintenance done, spacewalks, robotics and system work that the ground does all of the time. All of the objectives have to fit together so that there is no interference and that crew controller time is used efficiently. This takes a lot of work and a lot of

On the first day, campers learn about the missions they will complete at camp. Soon you'll know everything you need to know to be a space camp astronaut!

▲ Campers learn the details of their mission.

Tour of the Space Center

The towering rockets around Rocket Garden look like a forest of shiny white trees reaching high in the air. Some of them are the real rockets that flew in space. Others are models of the original rockets. Lots of planes are on display, too, because astronauts are also pilots. You can see an **F-16 Fighting Falcon** or a **MiG-15**. As a camper, you'll go on scavenger hunts through the park to find the different rockets and planes.

▲ The Rocket Garden needs to be big, because rockets take up a lot of room!

Inside the Space Center, exhibits and movies show the history of space travel. The *Saturn V* hangs above the floor. Visitors can walk under it and see how all the parts work. The *Saturn V* stands at over 36 stories tall.

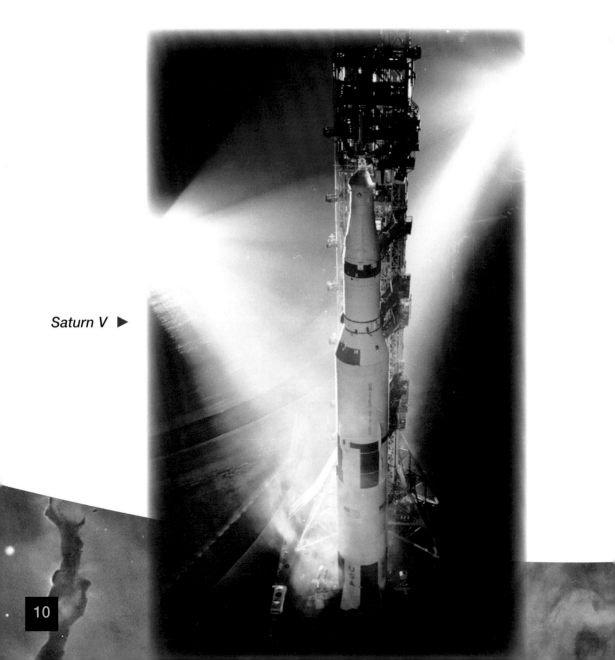

Saturn V ▶

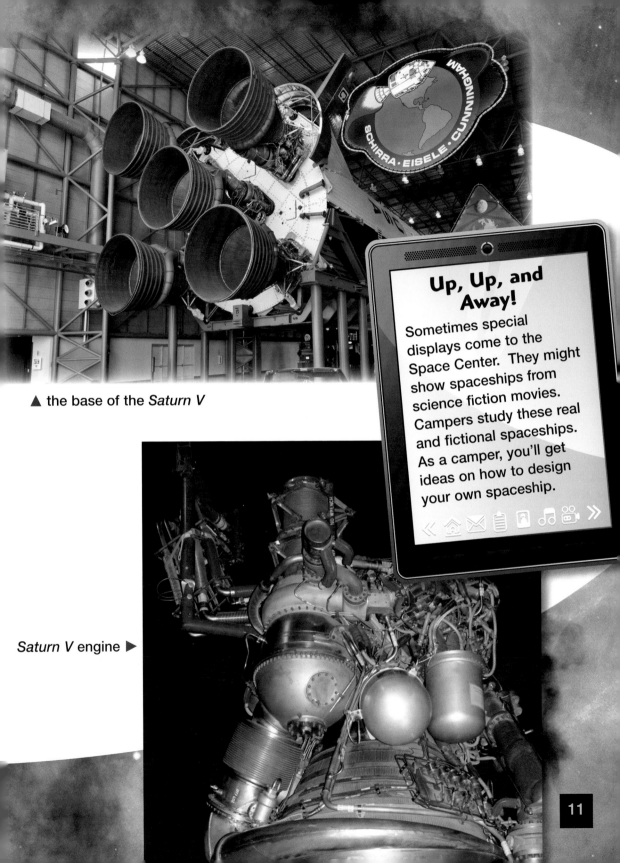

▲ the base of the *Saturn V*

Saturn V engine ▶

Up, Up, and Away!

Sometimes special displays come to the Space Center. They might show spaceships from science fiction movies. Campers study these real and fictional spaceships. As a camper, you'll get ideas on how to design your own spaceship.

Simulators

Space camp is home to amazing **simulators**. These machines let people feel as if they were in space without leaving Earth. You can see what liftoff really feels like. You can even feel your stomach drop from the **g-force**. Astronauts train with simulators every day to get used to the speed of space travel.

G-Force

G-force is a measurement of gravity. One "G" is equal to the feeling of gravity on Earth. Two Gs are two times the gravity on Earth.

▲ astronauts in a simulator

▼ a student in a flight simulator

Have you seen pictures of astronauts with their lunches floating around them? There is no **gravity** in space to give a sandwich weight, so it floats. Campers try out a simulator that lets them walk in every direction—even upside down! Astronauts also train underwater. That is the easiest way to feel weightless on Earth.

▼ training for gravity in space

Gravity

Gravity is a force that pulls objects to the ground. If we did not have gravity on Earth, we would float away. In space, gravity is much lower than on Earth. That's why you see astronauts floating around in the space shuttle.

Campers feel what it's like to tumble through space in the **5-Degrees of Freedom Chair.** It rolls forward, backward, and side to side. Astronauts practice moving in the chair. It helps them learn how to control their movements in space.

▲ 5-Degrees of Freedom Chair

Space Shuttle Speed

It takes six minutes for a space shuttle to go from 0–17,000 miles per hour. While orbiting Earth, the space shuttle travels at a speed of 17,500 miles per hour. When it's time to come home, the shuttle enters Earth's atmosphere at 16,700 miles per hour. After entering the atmosphere, the space shuttle slows down and lands between 200–230 miles per hour.

The $\frac{1}{6}$ **Gravity Chair** is a chair that lets people feel what it's like to walk on the moon. The moon's gravitational pull is $\frac{1}{6}$ the amount on Earth. That means if you weigh 100 pounds on Earth, you would only weigh about 17 pounds on the moon!

▲ trying the $\frac{1}{6}$ Gravity Chair

◀ footprint on the moon

In space, astronauts use the **Manned Maneuvering** (muh-NOO-ver-ing) **Unit** (MMU). This backpack unit is like a jet pack. It lets astronauts move in space without being tied to the shuttle.

◀ MMU in space

Kids of all ages can test the Manned Maneuvering Unit (MMU) at the Kids Space Place in Houston, Texas. ▼

Getting Hands-On

Astronauts have to rely on one another in space. That is what good teammates do. Campers also practice working together.

▲ International
   Space Station

Space Mission

The International Space Station (ISS) launched on November 23, 2002 from the Kennedy Space Center in Florida. It took many trips over many years to complete the space station. Every crew that visits the space station adds something new. The space station is always growing.

At space camp, you'll work in teams to build small rockets. Everyone works together to make them strong. These rockets have tiny passengers—bugs! Crickets, bees, and other insects act as astronauts. Commanders at mission control want to keep people safe when they travel into space. In the same way, campers want to keep these creatures safe.

Mission Control Center

Mission control runs the space shuttle missions from launch to landing. Many people work together at mission control to make sure the space shuttle is working properly.

Campers also perform experiments together. Your team leader may ask you to use **robotics**. A robot can explore a new world before people travel there. Can you work with your team to design a robot that could travel to Mars? Ready, set, go!

▼ Campers work together to build a robot.

Robotics

Robots are used in many different ways. In space, robots may be used to move very heavy things or explore planets humans cannot visit. New robots are being developed to help astronauts learn more about deep space.

Astronauts must be in good shape. It takes two hours of exercise in space to equal 20 minutes on Earth. Campers test their strength by climbing a rock wall or racing through a ropes course.

Campers spend much of their week learning the same skills astronauts do. However, astronauts train for many months to do a single task. Even simple actions, such as using a screwdriver, require practice. Astronauts must learn how to work wearing heavy suits, helmets, and gloves.

Water Training

Why do astronauts train underwater? When you are in water, you might feel as if you were floating. Heavy things feel very light in water. This is similar to what it feels like in space.

The Mission

You have been training all week. Now it's time to put on your flight suit. It's time for your mission! Some campers will be assigned to the ground crew. Others will be part of the flight crew. But you will all work together.

◀ Mission Specialist Kathryn D. Sullivan poses for a picture before putting on her space suit.

Primary Life Support Subsystem (PLSS)

Astronauts wear space suits to protect them when they are in space and on space walks. They weigh around 300 pounds and take about 45 minutes to put on. There are many different parts to a space suit. A very important part of the space suit is the Primary Life Support Subsystem (PLSS), which provides astronauts with many things they need to survive in space, such as water and oxygen.

Inside mission control, the ground crew counts down to lift off. Their screens show everything as if it were really happening outside. They put on their headphones and start talking with the **orbiter**. The rocket boosters **ignite** with a roar. We have lift off!

+00 00 08

▲ T-minus 8 seconds

Countdown to Launch

Do you know what happens at T-minus 0 seconds? A space shuttle lifts off and heads into space. The countdown clock for a shuttle launch begins at T-minus 43 hours and counting. Forty-three hours before a space shuttle lifts off, mission control performs hundreds of tests to make sure the shuttle is working properly. During the countdown, you may hear the test director say, "Holding." That means there is a pause in the countdown. A hold lets the countdown stay on schedule if a test takes longer than expected.

It is time to get to work. Space camp astronauts work together to change **solar panels** and refuel a supply tank. Others power up telescopes. They take pictures of planets.

◀ A boy looks through a powerful telescope to see deep into space.

Suddenly, your screen flashes red! A fuel hose has come loose. Will you have enough fuel to land? Will you have to **abort** the mission? You must think quickly to bring your crew home safely. Your week at space camp has taught you what to do. Together, the team is successful!

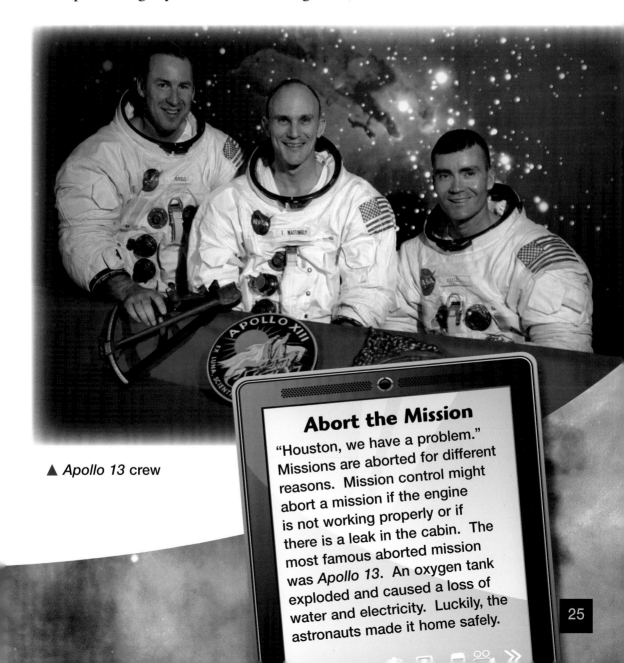

▲ *Apollo 13* crew

Abort the Mission

"Houston, we have a problem." Missions are aborted for different reasons. Mission control might abort a mission if the engine is not working properly or if there is a leak in the cabin. The most famous aborted mission was *Apollo 13*. An oxygen tank exploded and caused a loss of water and electricity. Luckily, the astronauts made it home safely.

Living in Space

The International Space Station allows people to live and work in space for six months at a time. Inside there are rooms called *modules*. Some rooms are for scientists to work in. Others are for sleeping or eating. Each living area has a sleeping bag that hooks to the wall.

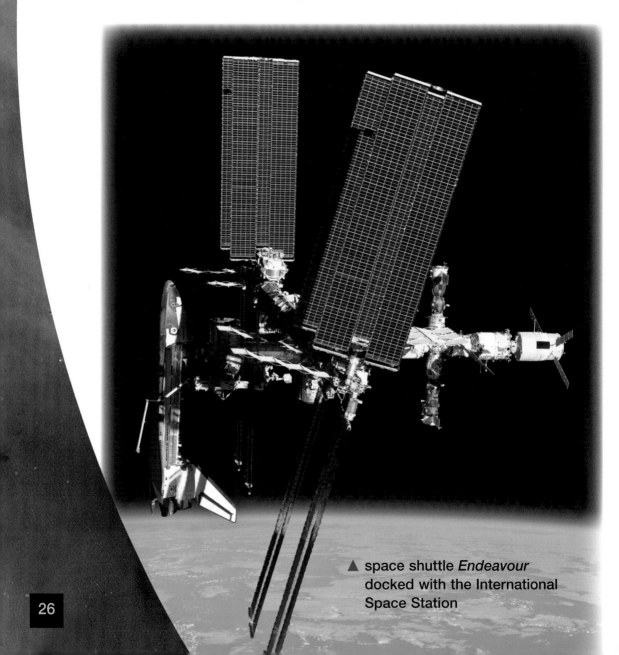

▲ space shuttle *Endeavour* docked with the International Space Station

In space, there is no up or down. So it does not matter where you sleep. Campers get to see what it's like to live in space when they visit the space station model.

◀ An astronaut rests in his sleeping bag aboard the International Space Station.

▼ Astronauts eat rice on Space Shuttle *Discovery*.

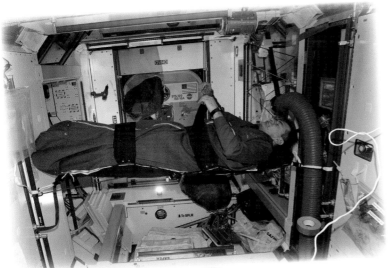

Space Food

Campers eat breakfast, lunch, and dinner, just like astronauts. In space, most food must be packaged a special way. To eat some food, astronauts add water. There are no refrigerators on a space shuttle, so food that must be kept cold is not taken into space.

In the future, people may be able to live on the moon. In the beginning, it will be very difficult. People will need to work hard to survive. To see what that would be like, campers pitch tents and sleep outside. Space camp is like outdoor camping in many ways.

▼ future space hotel room

Space Hotel

What if you could spend your summer vacation in space? A space hotel is being developed. It will be located about 200 miles above Earth. The hotel will have room for seven people and will cost about one million dollars for five days. Hotel guests will see 16 sunrises and sunsets every day and will orbit Earth once every hour and a half!

At the end of space camp, campers get to shake hands with an astronaut. He or she tells the campers to study science and dream big dreams. Years ago, the astronaut was a student just like you. Maybe you, too, will explore space one day!

▲ Children meet astronaut Leland Melvin.

Space Pilots

To become an astronaut, you must first train to be a jet airplane pilot. NASA's first astronauts were military jet pilots. They were called the *Original Seven*.

Glossary

$\frac{1}{6}$ **Gravity Chair**—a simulator that allows people to feel what it is like to walk on the moon

5-Degrees of Freedom Chair—a simulator that allows people to feel what it is like to move through zero-gravity space

abort—to abandon

astronaut—a person whose job it is to pilot, direct, or help on the crew of a spacecraft

F-16 Fighting Falcon—a 1976 American jet fighter plane

g-force—a measurement of gravity

gravity—a natural force that causes objects to be pulled toward each other

ignite—to set something on fire

launch—to put a vehicle into motion

Manned Maneuvering Unit (MMU)—a backpack unit for astronauts that acts like a jet pack

MiG-15—a jet fighter used by the the Soviet Union in 1949

orbiter—an object designed to orbit another object in space

planetariums—theaters that project images of stars and planets on a curved ceiling

robotics—the use of robots in different situations

simulators—systems or programs that re-create a task or experience

solar panels—groups of solar cells on flat panels, used to create electricity

Index

About the Author

Hillary Wolfe has been a writer throughout her adult life, mostly at newspapers and magazines. She was also a teacher for several years, working with students from kindergarten through high school as a literacy teacher and writing coach.

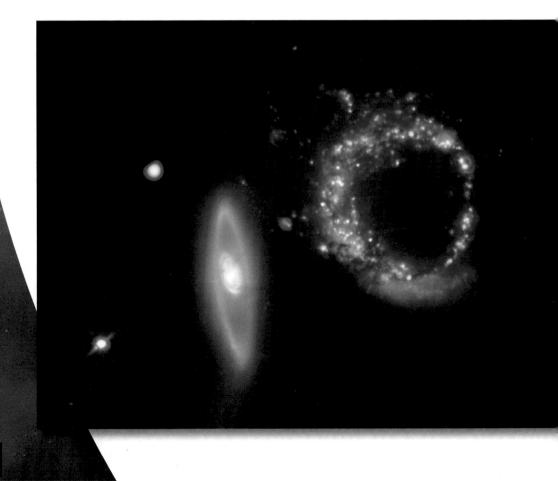